MAY -- 2019

Where in the World Can I . . .

SWIM WITH A MANTA RAY?

Where in the World Can I...

SWIM WITH A MANTA RAY?

WORLD BOOK

www.worldbook.com

World Book, Inc.
180 North LaSalle Street, Suite 900
Chicago, Illinois 60601
USA

For information about other World Book publications, visit our website at **www.worldbook.com** or call **1-800-WORLDBK (967-5325)**.

For information about sales to schools and libraries, call 1-800-975-3250 (United States), or 1-800-837-5365 (Canada).

© 2018 (print and e-book) by World Book, Inc. All rights reserved. No part of this publication may be reproduced, stored in a retrieval system, or transmitted in any form or by any means (electronic, mechanical, photocopying, recording, or otherwise) without written permission from World Book, Inc.

WORLD BOOK and the GLOBE DEVICE are registered trademarks or trademarks of World Book, Inc.

Library of Congress Cataloging-in-Publication Data for this volume has been applied for.

Where in the World Can I…
ISBN: 978-0-7166-2178-2 (set, hc.)

Swim with a Manta Ray?
ISBN: 978-0-7166-2187-4 (hc.)

Also available as:
ISBN: 978-0-7166-2197-3 (e-book)

Printed in China by Shenzhen Wing King Tong Paper Products Co., Ltd., Shenzhen, Guangdong
1st printing July 2018

STAFF

Writer: Grace Guibert

Executive Committee
President
 Jim O'Rourke

Vice President and Editor in Chief
 Paul A. Kobasa

Vice President, Finance
 Donald D. Keller

Vice President, Marketing
 Jean Lin

Vice President, International Sales
 Maksim Rutenberg

Vice President, Technology
 Jason Dole

Director, Human Resources
 Bev Ecker

Editorial
Director, New Print
 Tom Evans

Managing Editor, New Print
 Jeff De La Rosa

Senior Editor, New Print
 Shawn Brennan

Editor, New Print
 Grace Guibert

Librarian
 S. Thomas Richardson

Manager, Contracts & Compliance (Rights & Permissions)
 Loranne K. Shields

Manager, Indexing Services
 David Pofelski

Digital
Director, Digital Product Development
 Erika Meller

Manager, Digital Products
 Jonathan Wills

Graphics and Design
Senior Art Director
 Tom Evans

Coordinator, Design Development and Production
 Brenda Tropinski

Media Researcher
 Rosalia Bledsoe

Manufacturing/Production
Manufacturing Manager
 Anne Fritzinger

Proofreader
 Nathalie Strassheim

TABLE OF CONTENTS

- 6   What Is a Ray?
- 14   Manta Rays
- 26   Kona
- 32   Other Places to See or Swim with Manta Rays
    - Maldives
    - Great Barrier Reef
    - Manta Coast
- 44   Manta Rays Around the World
- 46   Books and Websites
- 47   Index
- 48   Acknowledgments

WHAT IS A RAY?

A ray is a type of fish. There are hundreds of kinds of rays. They are closely related to sharks—but they look much different!

cownose ray

guitarfish

stingray

Some types of rays are guitarfish, sawfish, skates, stingrays, eagle rays, electric rays, and manta rays.

Most rays have a flat body shaped like a dinner plate. Many have fins on their sides that look like wings! But rays come in many different shapes and sizes.

Most rays swim just above the sea floor, where they eat other fish and sea creatures that live near or on the bottom of the sea. The manta ray, a huge fish, swims in seawaters close to the surface. Some rays live deep in the ocean. But most live near the coast, where people can see and touch them!

Rays became an important part of many ancient cultures. Many groups of people in Peru, a South American country, showed stingrays in their pottery. The *Moche (MOH chay)* people of Peru worshipped the huge manta ray.

In ancient Greece, stingray *venom (VEHN uhm)*, or poison, was used by ancient dentists to numb people's mouths! The stingray has venom in one or two spines in its tail. When bothered, the stingray may swing its tail upward. This can inflict a painful wound on a person or other animal.

Ancient Romans may have used the shocks from electric rays to treat different illnesses! Two special *organs* (body parts) on the upper side of the fish's head allow it to give off electricity. Electric rays make these electric charges to defend themselves and to stun their *prey*, or animals they hunt. The shock from a full-grown electric ray can stun a human being!

Like sharks, rays have no bones inside their body. Instead, their skeleton is made of *cartilage (KAHR tuh lihj)*. Cartilage is tough, stretchy stuff that is softer and more flexible than bone. We have cartilage inside our ears and noses. Most other fish have skeletons made of bone, not cartilage.

Rays and sharks both have a body part called *gill slits*. All fish use *gills* to breathe in water. Gill slits are thin body openings that lead from the gills. A shark's gill slits are on the sides of its head. A ray's gill slits lie under its side fins, called *pectoral (PEHK tuhr uhl) fins*.

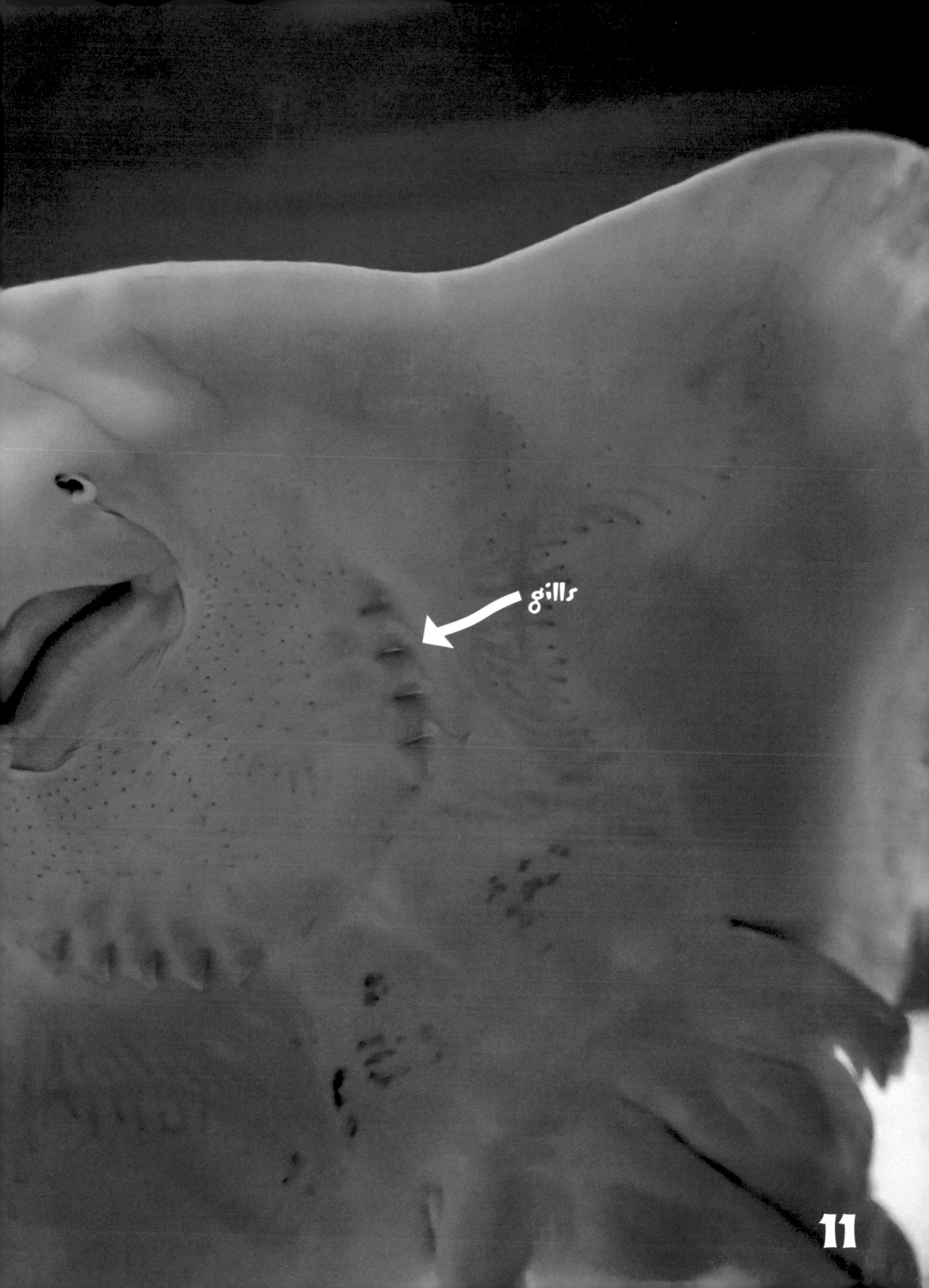

Rays give birth in a different way than most other fish. Most fish lay eggs that hatch later. But almost every kind of female ray hatches eggs inside her body. The female then gives birth to live young.

Rays are a unique and fascinating group of fish. While all rays share some features, one ray stands out from all the rest: the manta ray. These fish are gentle giants of the ocean!

MANTA RAYS

Manta rays are a huge type of ray. They get their special name because of their shape. *Manta* comes from the Spanish word for *cloak* or *blanket*.

Manta rays' pectoral fins stretch out on each side of their body like wings. This makes them look a bit like a blanket floating through the ocean waves! Manta rays swim through the water by flapping these fins.

Mantas have two fins on either side of their mouth. They look a bit like horns, so mantas are sometimes called *devilfish*. Even though that nickname sounds scary, manta rays are harmless to people.

Mantas have a short, skinny tail. Other rays, like stingrays, sometimes use their tail as a weapon. But manta ray tails are safe to touch!

There are two *(SPEE sheez)*, or kinds, of manta rays. The smaller species, called reef manta rays, grows to about 16 feet (5 meters) wide.

The larger species, called giant oceanic *(oh shee AN ihk)* manta rays, may grow up to 23 feet (7 meters) across!

Manta rays live in warm and tropical ocean waters all over the world. Each type of manta likes to live in a different area of the ocean. Giant oceanic manta rays live mostly in the open ocean. They swim toward waters that have lots of *plankton* to eat. Plankton are tiny living things that drift with the currents.

reef manta ray

Reef manta rays are found mostly in shallower waters close to shore. Reef mantas like to swim near *coral reefs.* Coral reefs are colorful, rocky mounds in the ocean. The reefs are made by tiny ocean animals called *corals.* The corals grow outer skeletons for protection. Over time, these skeletons form the reef. Coral grows in many shapes and many beautiful colors. Coral reefs make a place for many different animals to live.

Reef mantas are the type that people are more likely to see and swim with.

21

Manta rays weigh thousands of pounds or kilograms. The largest manta ray scientists have discovered weighed 6,000 pounds (2,700 kilograms)!

22

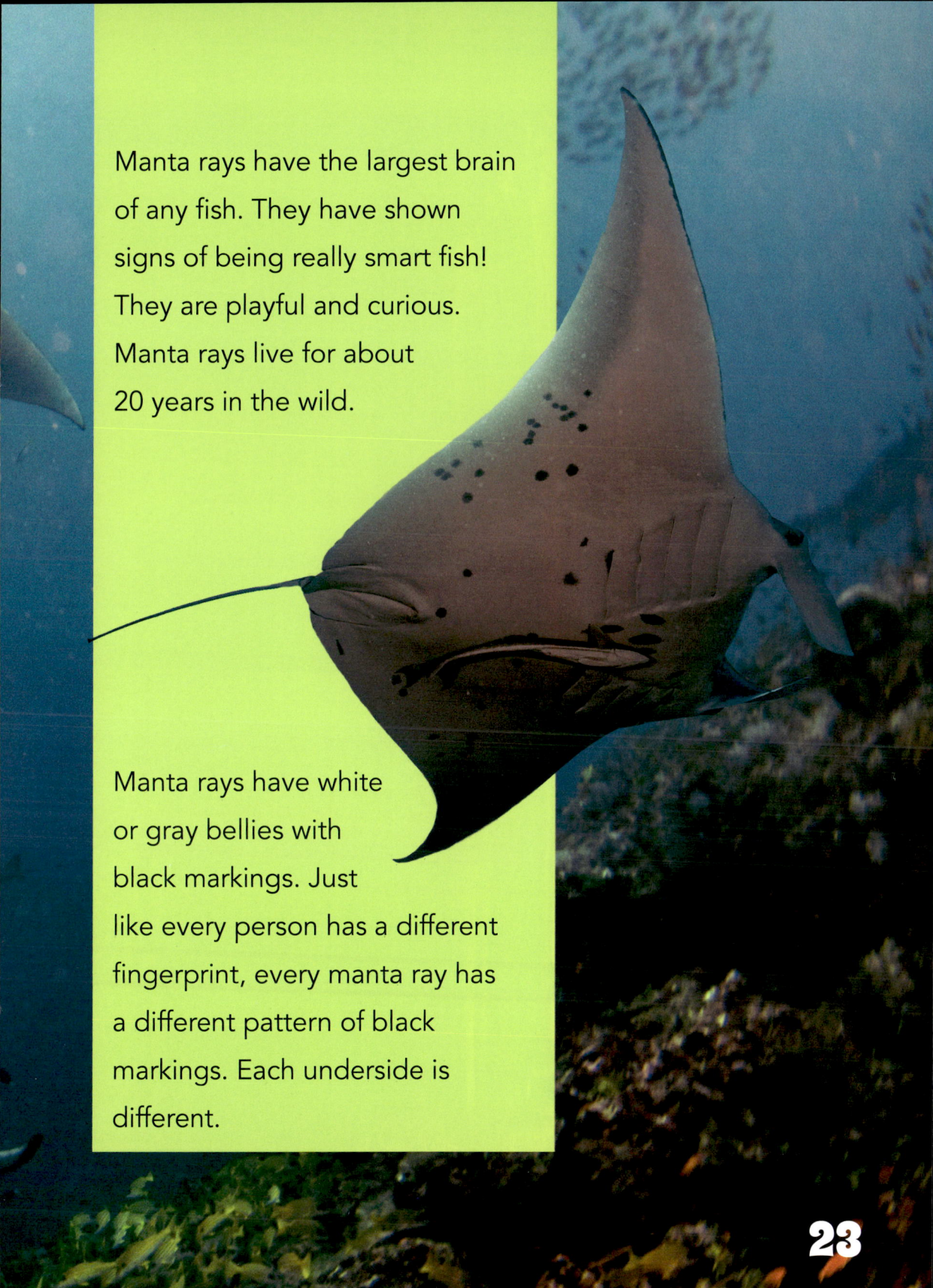

Manta rays have the largest brain of any fish. They have shown signs of being really smart fish! They are playful and curious. Manta rays live for about 20 years in the wild.

Manta rays have white or gray bellies with black markings. Just like every person has a different fingerprint, every manta ray has a different pattern of black markings. Each underside is different.

Both types of manta rays could be on their way to *extinction (ehk STIHNGK shuhn)*. Extinction is when a kind of living thing dies out completely. Pollution is damaging manta rays' homes. Fishermen sometimes pick up manta rays by accident. Some people hunt manta rays to eat their meat or to use their body parts as other products. It's important to do what we can to *conserve* (save) the ocean and the beautiful animals that live in it.

To swim with manta rays, you need to scuba *(SKOO buh)* dive or snorkel. Scuba diving uses special air tanks so people can breathe underwater. It requires plenty of training to stay safe.

Snorkeling allows swimmers to breathe through a tube while they stay near the surface. It does not take as much training as scuba diving. But swimmers should always be very careful for their own safety. Swimmers should also respect the animals and plants in the waters where they swim. Remember: this is THEIR home! We are the visitors!

Let's take a look at some places around the world where you can swim with manta rays!

KONA

One of the most unique manta ray dives takes place in Kona, Hawaii. Kona is a section of the Big Island of Hawaii. (Hawaii is a group of islands in the center of the North Pacific Ocean that is a U.S. state.)

Manta rays approach Kona to feed. And that's what makes this dive so special. Here, you can swim with manta rays as they eat dinner—at night!

26

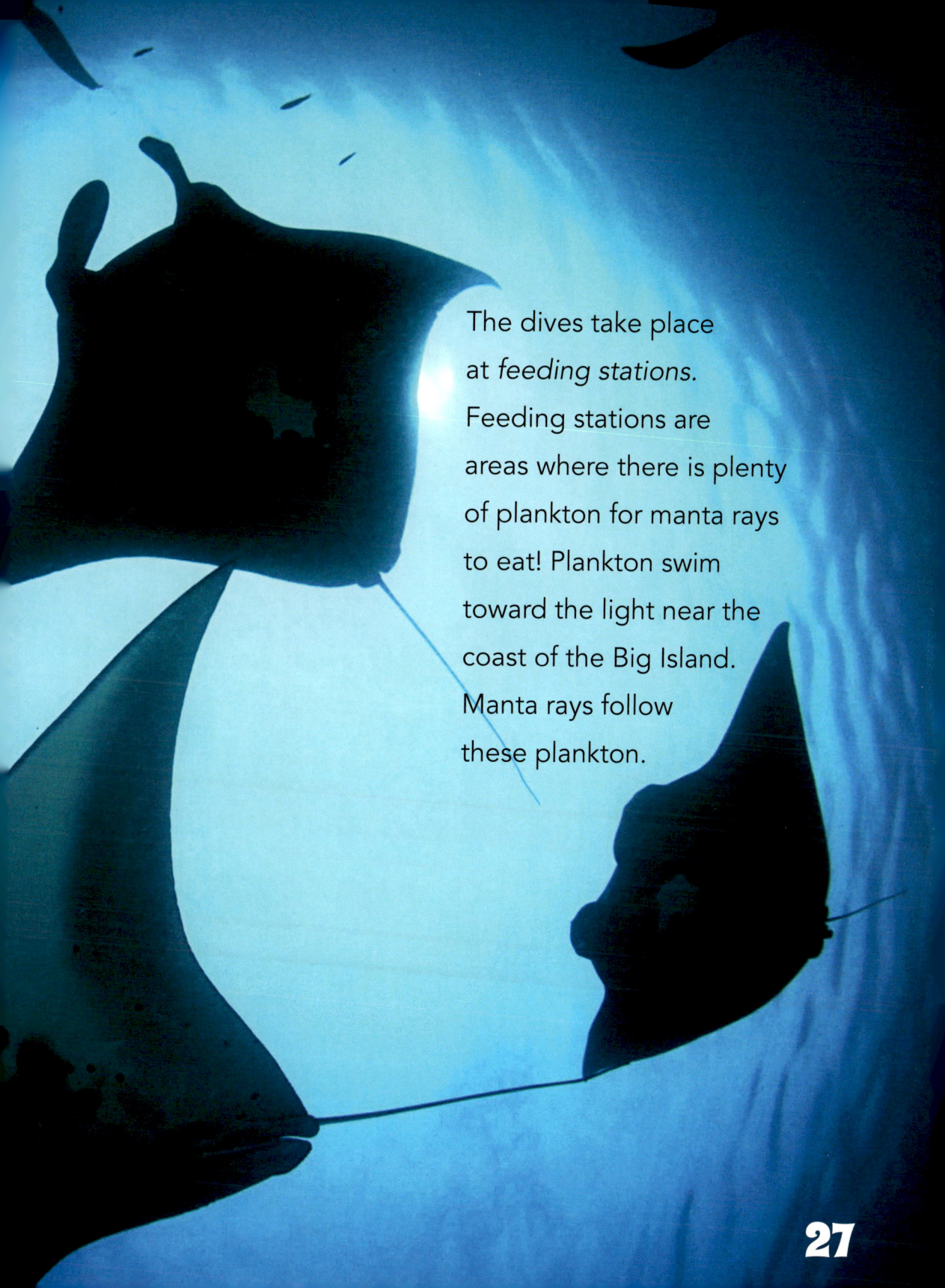

The dives take place at *feeding stations*. Feeding stations are areas where there is plenty of plankton for manta rays to eat! Plankton swim toward the light near the coast of the Big Island. Manta rays follow these plankton.

Manta rays swim through the water with their mouths open to gobble up their food. During a nighttime dive, you can see manta rays swim, flip, and somersault through the ocean waves.

A nighttime dive is magical and mysterious! The giant creatures are lit up by lights from the boat and the nearby beaches. As the manta rays swim through the dark water, divers can take in their beauty.

There are plenty of manta rays to be seen in Kona! In fact, parts of Kona have been nicknamed because of manta rays. Areas called Manta village and Manta heaven are common dive spots!

Kona also features the Manta Learning Center. Here, you can see photos and videos of manta rays in their natural *habitat* (home). The Learning Center also teaches visitors about the parts of a manta ray's body, its life cycle, its behavior, and how to protect manta rays.

But Kona isn't the only place to see mantas. There are popular places all over the world where you can see or swim with manta rays!

Other Places to See or Swim with Manta Rays

Maldives

Off the coast of the Maldives (*MAWL deevz* or *MAL dyvz*), an island country in the Indian Ocean, there are lots of reefs in the surrounding waters where mantas love to swim!

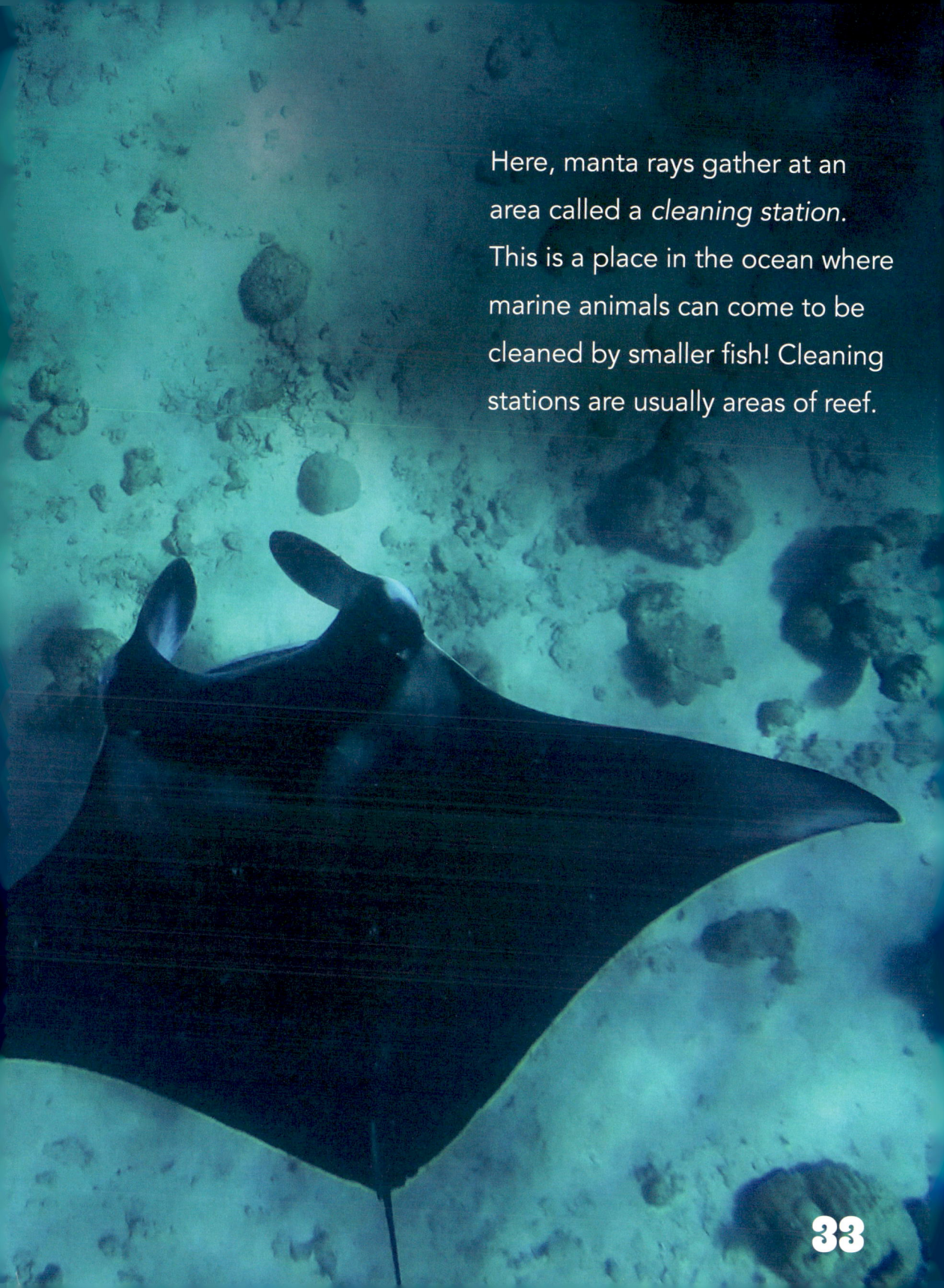

Here, manta rays gather at an area called a *cleaning station*. This is a place in the ocean where marine animals can come to be cleaned by smaller fish! Cleaning stations are usually areas of reef.

Small "cleaner fish" called *wrasses (ras ez)* like to clean manta rays! Cleaner wrasses pick off anything that has stuck to manta rays. They also eat any bits of food left over in manta rays' mouths! This helps both animals. The mantas get cleaned, and the wrasses get to eat!

At this cleaning station, manta rays swim just above the reef. They wait for cleaner wrasses to approach them. Mantas even line up to wait their turn for cleaning!

A swim off the coast of the Maldives is a great way to see mantas as well as the other ocean creatures they live with!

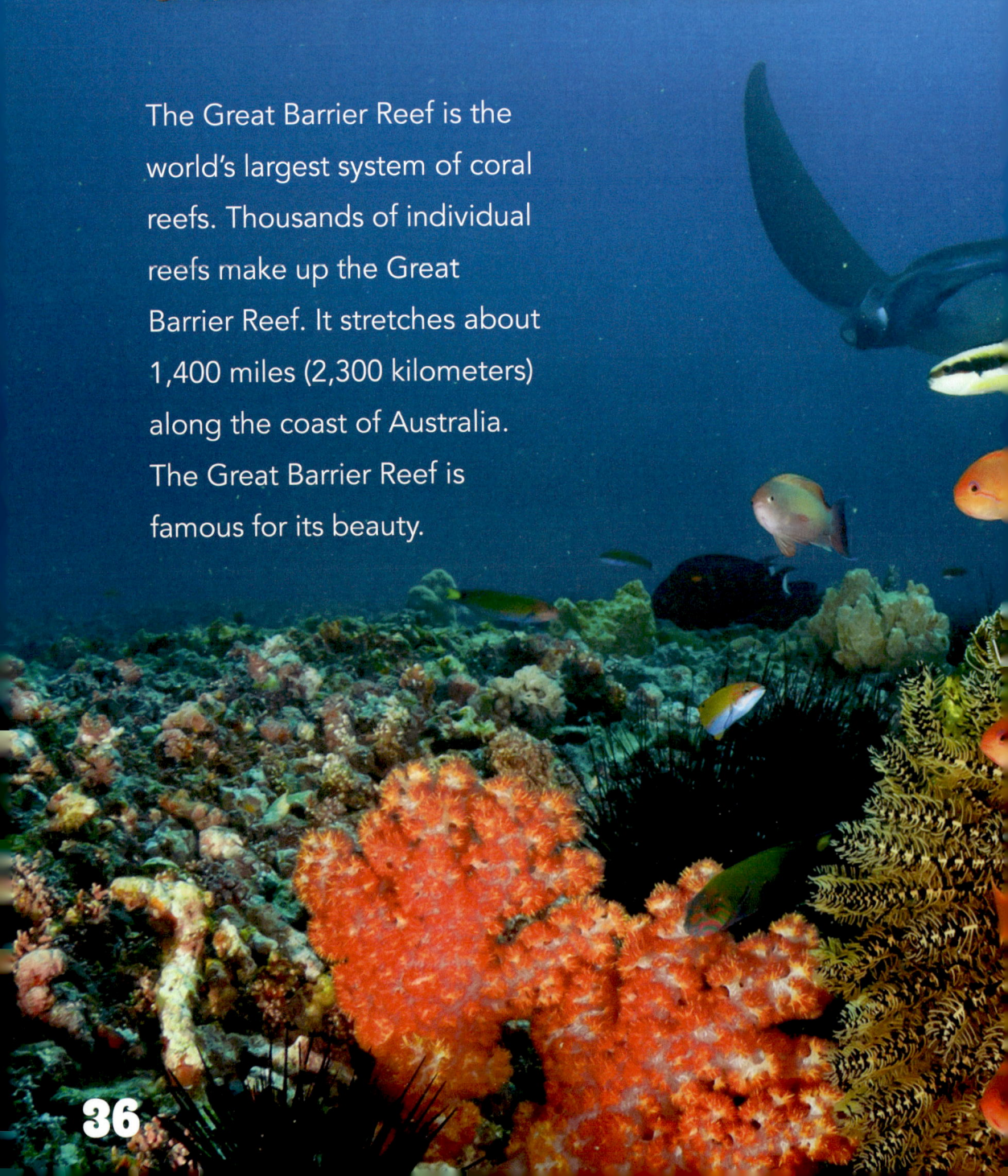

GREAT BARRIER REEF

The Great Barrier Reef is the world's largest system of coral reefs. Thousands of individual reefs make up the Great Barrier Reef. It stretches about 1,400 miles (2,300 kilometers) along the coast of Australia. The Great Barrier Reef is famous for its beauty.

Many types of ocean animals and plants live on its reefs. Hundreds of manta rays call the Great Barrier Reef home.

At Lady Elliot Island in the Great Barrier Reef Marine Park, you can see manta rays swim among some of the most beautiful plant and animal life in the world. Manta rays are protected within the park.

Today, the Great Barrier Reef is threatened by a process called coral *bleaching.* It is caused by *global warming,* a rise in Earth's average temperature. Unusually high water temperatures have caused many corals at the Great Barrier Reef to turn white and die. Scientists predict the continued bleaching will reduce the variety of corals at the reef and impact the creatures that depend on them. Since the 1980's, bleaching has affected about 50 percent of the Great Barrier Reef's corals.

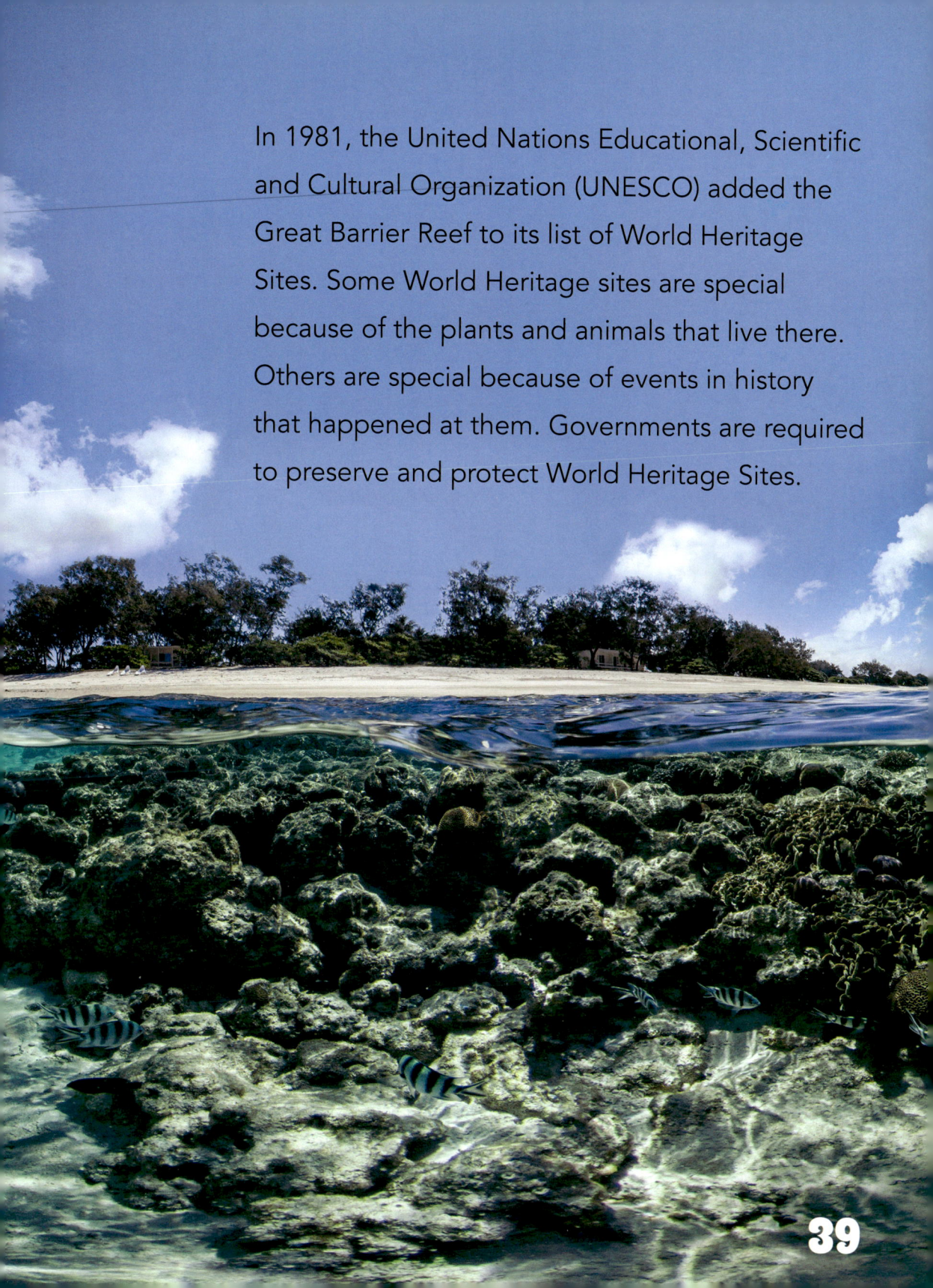

In 1981, the United Nations Educational, Scientific and Cultural Organization (UNESCO) added the Great Barrier Reef to its list of World Heritage Sites. Some World Heritage sites are special because of the plants and animals that live there. Others are special because of events in history that happened at them. Governments are required to preserve and protect World Heritage Sites.

MANTA COAST

Manta Coast is one of the most famous places to see manta rays. It is in southern Mozambique *(MOH zuhm BEEK)*, a country on the southeastern coast of Africa.

This area of the Indian Ocean has the largest number of manta rays. More than 500 manta rays live here!

41

Divers can head to Manta Reef, just off of Manta Coast, to swim with manta rays. Most dives near the Manta Reef allow divers to sit or stand on the ocean floor while mantas swim above or around them! This lets divers see the huge size of the manta rays.

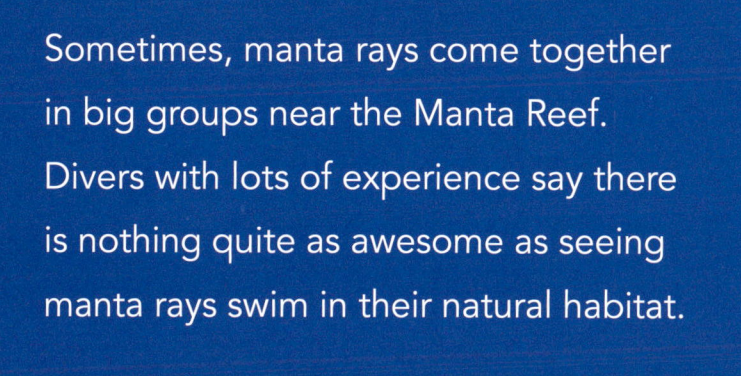

Sometimes, manta rays come together in big groups near the Manta Reef. Divers with lots of experience say there is nothing quite as awesome as seeing manta rays swim in their natural habitat.

MANTA RAYS AROUND THE WORLD

Manta rays swim in tropical waters all over the world. So there are plenty of areas to swim with manta rays. Other great dive sites include the Galapagos *(guh LAH puh gohs)* Islands, Indonesia, and Fiji *(FEE jee)*. The Galapagos Islands lie in the Pacific Ocean about 600 miles (970 kilometers) west of Ecuador *(EHK wuh dawr)*, a country in South America. Indonesia is a country in Southeast Asia. It is made up of more than 17,500 islands. Fiji is a country in the South Pacific Ocean. It is made up of more than 800 islands and reefs.

If you cannot make it to these places to dive or snorkel with manta rays, you can visit them and their ray relatives at aquariums around the world.

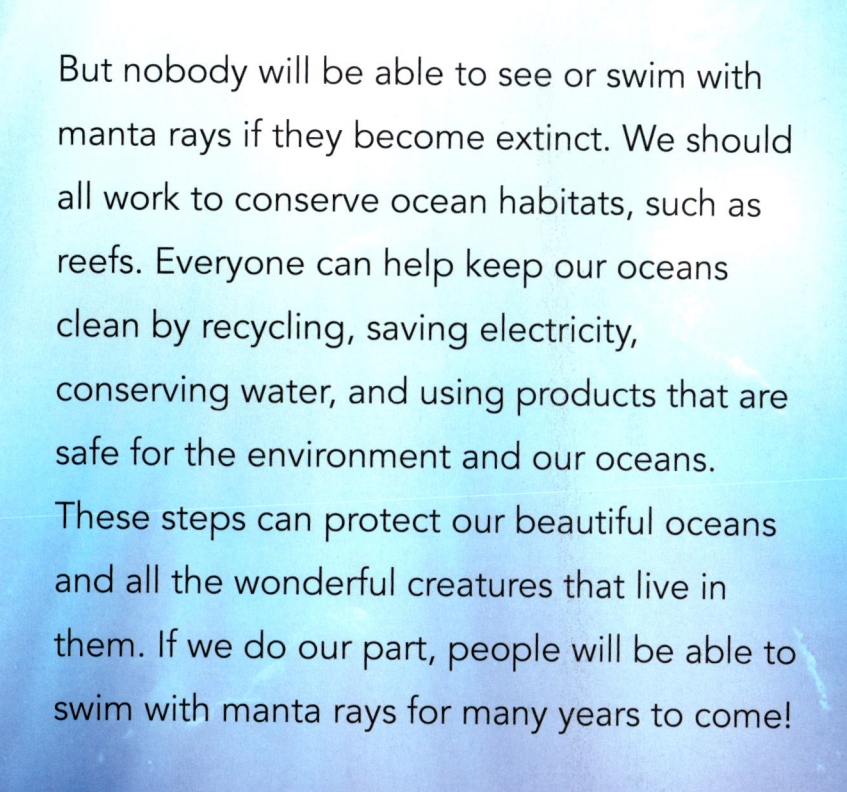

But nobody will be able to see or swim with manta rays if they become extinct. We should all work to conserve ocean habitats, such as reefs. Everyone can help keep our oceans clean by recycling, saving electricity, conserving water, and using products that are safe for the environment and our oceans. These steps can protect our beautiful oceans and all the wonderful creatures that live in them. If we do our part, people will be able to swim with manta rays for many years to come!

BOOKS AND WEBSITES

BOOKS

Manta Rays by Tori Miller (Powerkids PR, 2009)
This volume in a series called *Freaky Fish* teaches readers the manta ray basics. A glossary provides a comprehensive list of relevant terms to help young learners. It even includes a section of freaky facts!

Wings in the Water: The Story of a Manta Ray by Hope Irvin Marston (Soundprint, 1998)
Follow the adventure of one manta ray as it tries to escape danger in the Philippine Sea! This book, from the Smithsonian's *Oceanic Collection* series, provides important information about manta rays in the context of an engaging fictional plot. The story also brings attention to a danger that threatens manta rays—fishermen—and the importance of conserving the beautiful animal.

Manta Rays by Colleen A. Sexton (Bellwether Media, 2009)
This volume of the *Blastoff! Readers: Oceans Alive* series is well suited for younger readers (grades 2-3). Filled with beautiful photos, *Manta Rays* teaches about the graceful animal in approachable terms.

WEBSITES

Manta Ray Advocates
http://www.mantarayshawaii.com/mantaexperience.html

Information about manta rays and diving with them in Kona.

Manta Ray World
http://www.mantaray-world.com/

This website includes facts and information on manta rays, including different species, habitat, feeding, anatomy, evolution, predators, conservation, and interaction with humans.

Manta Trust
http://www.mantatrust.org/

This website is dedicated to conservation of manta rays through research, awareness, and education. Includes detailed information about manta rays and where they are found. Includes a guide and video on how to swim with manta rays.

INDEX

Australia, 36

brains, 23

cartilage, 10
cleaning stations, 33–35
conservation, 24, 45
coral bleaching, 38
coral reefs, 20–21, 32, 33, 35. See also Great Barrier Reef; Manta Reef
corals, 21

devilfish, 16

eagle rays, 7
eggs, 12
electric rays, 6, 7, 9
extinction, 24, 45

feeding stations, 27
Fiji, 44
fins, 10, 15–16

Galapagos Islands, 44
giant oceanic manta rays, 18–20
gill slits, 10
global warming, 38

Great Barrier Reef, 36–39
Greece, ancient, 9
guitarfish, 6, 7

Hawaii, 26

Indian Ocean, 32, 41
Indonesia, 44

Kona, Hawaii, 26–31

Lady Elliot Island, 38

Maldives, 32–35
Manta Coast, 40–43
Manta Learning Center, 31
manta rays, 6, 7, 9, 13–25
Manta Reef, 42–43
Moche people, 9
Mozambique, 40

ocean habitats, 34

pectoral fins, 10, 15
Peru, 9
plankton, 20, 27
pollution, 24

rays, 6–13
reef manta rays, 18, 20–21
Rome, ancient, 9

sawfish, 7
scuba diving, 25
sharks, 6, 10
skates, 7
snorkeling, 25
stingrays, 7, 9
swimming with manta rays, 21, 25, 44–45
   in the Great Barrier Reef, 36–39
   in Kona, 26–31
   in the Maldives, 32–35
   at Manta Coast, 40–43

tails, 17

UNESCO, 39

venom, 9

World Heritage Sites, 39
wrasses, 34

47

ACKNOWLEDGMENTS

Cover: © Rich Carey, Shutterstock;
© Chainarong Phrammanee, Shutterstock

2-25 © Shutterstock

26-27 Courtesy of Liquidhawaii.com

28-37 © Shutterstock

38-39 Aaron Spence, The Ocean Agency/ XL Catlin Seaview Survey (licensed under CC BY-SA 3.0)

40-41 © Shutterstock

42-43 Steve Dunleavy (licensed under CC BY 2.0)

44-45 © Shutterstock